The SERVANT *of All*

*If any man desire to be first, the same shall be
last of all, and servant of all.—Mark 9:35*

DR. KENNETH BARBOUR

ISBN 978-1-63874-484-9 (paperback)
ISBN 978-1-63874-858-8 (hardcover)
ISBN 978-1-63874-485-6 (digital)

Christian Faith Publishing
832 Park Avenue
Meadville, PA 16335
www.christianfaithpublishing.com

Printed in the United States of America

DEDICATION

To my wife, Joyce Elaine Barbour, who passed away on March 16, 2001. Faithfulness, fidelity, and loyalty were her trademarks, and she was the epitome of the virtuous woman as described in Proverbs 31:10–31.

I consider myself the most fortunate man in the world to have had the privilege of having her as my soul mate for thirty-seven years. She was willing to accept my faults, failures, and shortcomings and to still love me with all of her heart.

My greatest appreciation of her was her steadfast love for Jesus Christ and her steadfast support of me in spiritual and educational pursuits, especially through the demands of the dissertation process as I pursued my doctorate. She was forgiving, patient, kind, gracious, and understanding and a wonderful mother to our three daughters.

I have every confidence that we will be reunited in heaven, a place of perfect happiness—one of our greatest joys will be our reunion with those we love, and God will not withhold that joy from us!

A STORY WRITTEN
FOR GOD'S GLORY

"I will instruct you and teach you in the way
you should go; I will advise you with
my loving eye on you." (Psalm 32:8)

ALL GLORY BELONGS TO GOD the Father, Son, and Holy Spirit because God is the source and the strength of all the good we do. I pray that God will bring to Himself glory and honor as I seek to use the gifts God has given me to bless the readers of my book. I thank Him for being my strength, guide, and wisdom so that I have finally been able to accomplish the writing of my book. All glory to God forever and ever. Amen.

ACKNOWLEDGMENT

"Perfume and incense bring joy to the heart, and the pleasantness of a friend springs from their heartfelt advice." (Proverbs 27:9)

To Alan Ciechanowski, my friend and brother in the Lord.

Writing a book is harder than I thought and more rewarding that I could have imagined. I thank you for the countless hours and days spent editing draft pages, advising, communicating with the publisher and designing the front cover of the book. It is because of your efforts, encouragement, and ongoing support that I have a legacy to pass on to my family and friends. None of this would have been possible without you.

"A good friend is a blessing from God." (I Samuel 18:3)

To Bernice Fink, my friend and sister in the Lord.

Thank you for giving of your time and writing skills in making my early years become a reality. It was heart rendering to read of my early years wearing shoes with cardboard to keep my feet dry. Years later while wearing my Nice 97 walking shoes on a "Dress Down Day" a student remarked, "I like your kicks." It made my day to think that I no longer would have cardboard to keep my feet dry!

It is evident that Ken is an education leader who brings a vison for excellence to his call. I had the pleasure to work with Ken while forming an articulation to provide students at the Harty Bible School an opportunity to enter Geneva College on advanced standing. He demonstrates patience and wisdom in very difficult situations and most importantly he is a man of integrity and moral commitment.

John H. White, President Geneva College (1987)

***

My visit to your school, your enthusiasm as well as your attitude, was the highlight of my trip to Pittsburgh. Your Superintendent is truly fortunate to have a principal like you.

Yvette de Prado, Ph.D, Superintendent
Cupertino Union School District (1985)

***

The Manchester Citizens Corporation Board and staff wants you to know that Manchester's first place showing in "NeighborFair '88" happened only because you took the time to care. Thank you for being one of the very few special persons at our booth to tell Pittsburgh about a great place to live: our home, Manchester.

Stanley Lowe, CEO Manchester Citizens Corporation (1988)

***

As an administrator in the Pittsburgh Public School, Dr. Barbour is legendary in this region. As a new principal of West Side Academy, Dr. Barbour was faced with perhaps one of the most daunting challenges in the Pittsburgh school district. Fairywood Elementary School was considered a disaster zone—a lost cause. It had sunk to one of the lowest academically rated elementary schools in the district, and due to its proximity to a public housing project the school was dangerous for children and teachers alike. Dr. Barbour's leadership paid spectacular dividends with much improved test results, proud children, and the respect of parents, teachers, and those who once skeptically held scant hope for the school's success. The school was made safe, pride reentered the learning community and children began to thrive in an emotional and physically secure environment, and a waiting list of hopeful parents anxious to become part of an exciting school experience.

Dr. Barbour is at educator leader who has carved a national reputation for himself and has won the respect of teachers, researchers, and most importantly the children he has helped in his distinguished career in the schools.

Timothy Rusnak, Ph.D (1996) Professor, Duquesne University

***

I have had the distinct pleasure of knowing Dr. Kenneth Barbour over the past six years that my daughter attended Hillcrest Christian Academy. In my many discussions and interactions with Dr. Barbour as Principal of Hillcrest, I have come to know him as a remarkably capable, gracious, warm but firm, and creative school administrator of the very highest caliber. His vast knowledge, experience, vitality and troubleshooting genius are worthy of my highest, unqualified recommendation for him as a school principal and person.

In my professional life I have had occasion to represent a number of school districts, and interact extensively with many fine school administrators; however, I have yet to come across one that can match the ability and character of Dr. Barbour. He is the finest school principal I have ever met."

Nicholas Wininsky Attorney at Law Wininsky Law Offices (2010)

***

When an individual reads the title of a new book, not often can his or her next thought be: "That is true!" In Dr. Ken Barbour's case, however the title of new book, "The Servant of All", helps us identify, understand, and appreciate the strength, the educational leadership capacity, and the integrity that has undergirded Dr. Barbour's work throughout his career in schools in this region of Pennsylvania.

I have known Dr. Barbour since he was an exemplary graduate in the School of Education, University of Pittsburgh 1979-1984. Over the ensuing years, I have been pleased to observe his determination to provide: 1) high quality learning and character education opportunities for students, K-Grade 12. 2) professional development opportunities for teachers and administrators at all levels; and 3) opportunities for parents and members of the community to engage in the vital role of support for quality education for all students.

Ask Dr. Barbour to tell you what has contributed to his success, and he will be quick to say that his parents helped him understand the importance of giving to others and the value of intrinsic—not extrinsic—rewards in your heart. Many children and countless adults are grateful for the constant care and commitment shown to them through their association with him.

Dr. Ken Barbour is a man of expert knowledge, insightful wisdom, and strong faith. The integration of these personal qualities has been demonstrated in his life as he has served as an educator whose passion is the education of children and youth to be contributors to our society.

Kathryn S. Atman, Ph.D Emeritus Faculty School
of Education University of Pittsburgh (2021)

***

When evaluating a company, a sports team (the Steelers have employed three coaches over the past 45 years) or a school, stability in leadership is critical. When my children attended Manchester

Elementary School, the building had two principals in 20 years. My son's first grade principal, Dr. Ken Barbour, came to his high school graduation to shake his hand and congratulate him. That dedication and stability from the school's leadership is critical if we hope to turn some of our troubled schools around.

Lawrence Ehrich, Chairman of the Board, Northside Conference Education Committee.(1-23-15)

***

Dr. Barbour made my last year as a student at Harty Bible School (2003) a year I shall never forget. As my teacher for the Deuteronomy/Joshua Class he taught the class with in-depth understanding of Scripture (II Timothy 2:15). He knew each one of his students in a personal way and he inspired me to strive for excellence with every test. He also saw potential in me appointing me to teach the Teachers Training Class and the Deuteronomy/Joshua Class at HBS. To this day I am using the same method of teaching he used. When I get accolades from the students, I tell them that I owe it all to Dr. Barbour!

Minister Bernice E. Carson (2021)

CHAPTER 1

The Early Years

ORN AND RAISED IN OAKDALE, a rural community west of
Pittsburgh, I was the tenth of thirteen children—seven boys and
six girls. It was because of our shared childhood experiences and the
godly influence of our parents that we became successful in life.

My father was a coal miner. He walked two to three miles each
way every day to the coal mine in a nearby community. My mother
was a domestic worker who cleaned neighborhood houses and laundered for families in our community, all while caring for and providing for her household at the same time.

My sister Virginia was already 17 years old when I was born
and actually served as midwife when my mother gave birth to me.
It proved to be the beginning of her career, as she later served as an
army nurse during World War II, and eventually became head nurse
at St. Luke's Hospital in New York.

Our house did not have running water, so we had to carry water
from a well pump in the cellar to the kitchen, where it would be
used for several purposes. We would take turns with a dipper to get a
drink from one bucket of fresh water. Another bucket of water would
be used for cooking and to wash the dishes. On Saturday nights, a
bucket of water was placed on top of the potbelly stove to heat for
our weekly baths, and we took turns bathing in a large galvanized
metal tub. We had no indoor bathroom facilities, so my father built a
small enclosed structure that had one or two holes in a seat built over
a pit to serve as an outdoor toilet. We had "potties" placed beside our
beds for nighttime use and took turns washing our faces and hands

each morning using a wash basin. My mother would spend several weekdays hand-washing clothes in a washing tub and hanging them on the line outside to dry.

We used the potbelly stove to heat the rooms because we did not have a furnace to heat the entire house. It was a cast-iron wood-burning stove, round with a bulge in the middle.

The "ice man" came to our neighborhood once a week to deliver blocks of ice which were placed in the upper part of the icebox to keep food cold. During mild winter months, we would place milk and food items outside to keep them cold. During the colder snowier months, we gathered clean snow in a bowl, and Mother would use it to make us an ice cream treat.

My childhood home in Oakdale

It was a scary time for me during World War II when our country practiced air raid drills to make our town invisible to enemy bombers. A siren would go off, and our neighborhood became completely darkened. I was worried that enemy planes were going to drop poisonous gas bombs on us.

We didn't go out to eat like people do these days. We stayed at home and ate together as a family. Mother made delicious "one-pot meals." To make vegetable soup, she would add potatoes, tomatoes, onions, celery, carrots, and corn all together in one pot.

Though poor, my siblings and I enjoyed playing together using our imaginations and creativity. We built four-wheeled carts using wooden boxes and pretended they were actual cars. There were only a few households that had a television, so we listened to an old Atwater Kent radio. We liked to sing when my father played the family piano. At other times, we created our own tunes on the piano.

At Christmastime, my brothers Clifford and Roger, my sisters Elaine, Frances, and Arlene and I shared one toy each among ourselves, and we had candy that was given to us at Sunday school. My family could not afford to buy a Christmas tree. However, Roger and I wanted one for our younger brother and sisters, so we found a way to obtain one. Stores would throw unsold trees into a creek that ran on the edge of town at the end of each evening. Roger and I waded into the creek, grabbed a Christmas tree, and dragged it to our house. We decorated it with paper stars, angels, ornaments, and Christmas trinkets, all of which were handmade in our art classes at school.

There is a very special place in my heart for memories of the fun times we enjoyed as kids while playing at a water tower (better known as "the tank") at the end of

My brother Roger and I, circa 1998.

our street. Being oblivious to the tank's true purpose, we had the best of times running around the tank playing tag, and we looked forward to the summer months when the tank would overflow so that we could put our bathing trunks on and stand under the cool water that spilled over the edge.

15

Making Ends Meet

There were challenges that played an important role in who we were to become. Battles between rival coal mining unions led to strikes, and several times throughout the year, my father would be on strike and subsequently without an income. These strikes imposed a major financial challenge, and there were threats of foreclosure on our house. Sheriff sale signs were put up on several properties in the community. Late one night, Roger and I walked through the town ripping the signs from the posts. Thankfully, we were not arrested. Eventually, my father worked out a deal with the bank to begin paying small amounts of rent, which were later converted to house payments. When money was tight, I remember wearing shoes with holes in the bottom and putting cardboard inside to keep my feet dry on rainy days.

Roger and I worked various jobs in our community to help with household expenses. We worked on Saturdays as delivery boys for Victor's Community Market (now Sil's); we delivered newspapers for Tommy Dodds, the owner of Oakdale Pharmacy; we shined shoes at Mr. Gregory's Shoe Repair Shop; and we even picked blackberries and walked up and down the street selling them to our neighbors. The Greater Pittsburgh International Airport was built in the early 1950s and provided many jobs, so Roger and I worked there after school and on weekends.

Roger and I worked here when it was Victor's

Discrimination

We had to learn to deal with discrimination during the early years. For example, African-Americans at that time were prohibited from going to Kennywood Park, so we used our creativity by carrying sucker rods home from an oil well, joining them together to make roller coaster tracks, and using orange crates as roller coaster cars. Going to the Grand Theater in McDonald with my white classmates and friends meant being separated from them in the theater and having to sit in the section designated for Negroes. But afterward, we would walk home together and discuss the movie.

Roger, Elaine and I learned to play instruments while in elementary school and played all through high school. During the summer months, the Oakdale Fire Department Band marched in parades and performed in several communities during the summer carnivals. The mayor of the town, "Happy" Dunbar, issued an order that Negro teenagers would not be allowed to participate. So two African-American men, Melville Campbell and Emmitt Carter from McDonald organized a marching band just for the young boys of their race. On Sunday afternoons after church, they drove to our town and picked us up for band practice. We marched every year in the Emancipation Day parade held in McDonald.

Due to the prohibition of black children from swimming in neighborhood and county swimming pools, my siblings and I would swim in an abandoned strip mine pit that contained water up to a depth of one hundred feet or more. We didn't realize how dangerous it was until the day my brother had to save me from

The oil well from which we gathered sucker rods to make our own roller coasters.

drowning. I had jumped off a rock ledge into a part of the strip mine that appeared to be a smooth area of water. Its appearance, however, proved to be deceiving. Strong undercurrents began pulling me under the water. Only through the swift and courageous help of my brother Roger was I able to make it back to dry land.

My sisters' school friends and neighborhood playmates were active Girl Scouts in the community; however, Elaine, Frances, and Arlene were not permitted to become Scouts because of discriminatory community-based bylaws. Roger and I were the first to break the color barrier by becoming members of a Boy Scout troop. This change was made by scoutmaster Bob Keenan in the midst of opposition from community leaders.

My brother and I were the first to break the color barrier by becoming Boy Scouts. This was our cabin.

Whenever a family member or friend passed away, the funeral homes in the area would not accommodate black people. Instead, accommodations for grieving families were made by African-American funeral directors such as Quinn Banks in Washington, PA. The body of the deceased was placed in the family home for viewing. In our town, burial was in the "black section" of the Oakdale cemetery.

Even though my sister Virginia was valedictorian of an all-white senior high school class, she was denied acceptance into the University of Pittsburgh's School of Nursing.

Although laws at that time may have been discriminatory, many people in our lives were not. A neighbor, Albert McIntyre, drove my seriously ill mother to Mercy Hospital and he drove her home after she spent a week there. My dad did not have a car, so this was a special blessing and favor.

My parents could not afford to buy a turkey for our Thanksgiving dinner. Early on one Thanksgiving Day, Roger and I went to the farm of our teacher, Mrs. Ethel McGill, who gave us two prepared chickens for our Thanksgiving meal.

The Oakdale Pharmacy, owned and operated by Tommy and Dolly Dodds, did not discriminate. We enjoyed sitting in the old wooden booths with our classmates enjoying a cold Coca-Cola while talking about school events.

Though we were discriminated against at times, my parents taught us never to harbor hatred in our hearts toward those who were imposing the policies and carrying them out. My parents' wise teaching has carried me through my entire lifetime and has enabled me to succeed, to love others, and to touch many lives of all races.

My mother, Evon

My mother had a major influence on my life, and she held us to high Christian and moral standards. Chapter 31 of the book of Proverbs speaks of the attributes of a godly woman that parallel the life of my mother:

"She seeks wool, and flax, and works willingly with her hands. She lays her hands to the spindle and her hands hold the distaff" (Proverbs 31:13 NKJV). My mother had an old-fashioned Singer sewing machine that did not run by electricity. She used the sewing machine to make dresses for herself and skirts for the girls. She would even repair rips in my jeans.

"She rises also while it is yet night and giveth meat to her household" (Proverbs 31:15 NKJV). Mother would rise early to prepare hot cereal for us before leaving for school. The cereal was made of corn meal mixed with water or milk, called mush or porridge.

"She considers a field and buys it, with her hands she planted a vineyard" (Proverbs 31:16 NKJV). I don't know that my mother ever bought a field, but she certainly helped plant a garden every year. And in the early fall, she would be busy canning blackberries, corn, tomatoes, and green beans.

"She is not afraid of the snow for her household, for all her household are clothed" (Proverbs 31:21 NKJV). I remember the quilts mother made so we could cuddle up and keep warm during cold winter nights. Her manual sewing machine made a lot of noise—like an old car engine on its last leg.

"Her children rise up and call her blessed" (Proverbs 31:28 NKJV). When I think of my mother being crowned with years, how her wise counsel, loving discipline, and holy example inspired me to train my children as I myself had been trained, I will never cease to call her "blessed" and to thank God for her—His invaluable gift to a family of thirteen children.

My father, George

My father's name was George, a name derived from the Greek word *georgos*, meaning "farmer." As time went on, I came to realize and appreciate the endurance it required of my father to provide enough food for a family of thirteen by raising crops, poultry, and other animals, in addition to working in the coal mine. Producing a good crop to feed his family was his main goal. Dad would have us plant a large garden in the spring and summer with tomatoes, onions, potatoes, corn, and green beans. I also remember going into the fields with my brothers and sisters to pick dandelion greens for a meal.

One of my earliest memories was being assigned the relentless task of watering the garden and picking weeds while Dad was at work. My daily routine included feeding the chickens and pigs before going to school, repeating the same chores after school, adding in any work needed in the garden, and then completing homework before bedtime.

Life was hard work, but later in life, I came to realize that our family life of gardening was about a family pulling together to make things work with limited funds and resources, and with many sacrifices. Now I understand why my father was always working on something in the yard.

The coal mine owners provided stores, referred to as the "company store," where the miners could purchase necessities for themselves and their families. My family bought salt, pepper, cornmeal, flour, tea, and sugar from the store. Miners were paid little for their back-breaking labor and sometimes could not afford the basic necessities of life.

The company store gave the miners credit to help support their families, and I remember times when my father would come home on payday with an empty check because the credit purchases at the company store exceeded the amount of his pay. The verse "I owe my soul to the company store" from the Tennessee Ernie Ford song "Sixteen Tons" takes on a special meaning to me because of this.

My father not only worked tirelessly to provide faithfully for his family, but he was also known for helping others in his community whenever he could throughout his life. In my dad's later years, I had the pleasure of listening as he shared his deep memories of the past. The retelling actually made him smile. His stories made me feel that I would have liked to have lived in those times.

> Our father kept a garden,
> a garden of his heart.
> He planted all the good things
> that gave our lives a start.
> He turned us to the sunshine,
> and encouraged us to dream,
> Fostering and nurturing
> the seeds of self-esteem.
> And when the winds and rain came,
> he protected us enough,
> But not too much because he knew
> we'd need to stand up strong and tough.

21

His constant good example
always taught us right from wrong.
Markers for our pathway
that will last a lifetime long.
We are our father's garden, and we are his legacy.
Thank you, Dad. We love you!

Author Unknown

What the Rich Young Ruler and I have in common

Our family attended Trimble Chapel AME Zion church, a small African-American church where we actively attended Sunday school, church services, and a Sunday evening "Christian endeavor class." We faithfully attended and participated in the choir and church youth groups with inner-city young people. My baptism at twelve years of age began my spiritual walk with God, which led to a lifetime of fulfilling Christian ministry. As a child, I acted as pastor and conducted a funeral and burial for our family pet that had died. When my sisters' baby dolls became ragged and deteriorated and they received new ones, I was the pastor conducting the burial under a tree in our yard for the ones declared as being passed away.

Standing with the "church mother," Sister Carrie Fuqua

All these childhood experiences shaped my life and led to a lifetime in the fields of Christian ministry, teaching in public schools, and in a Christian adult Bible school. My administration skills prepared me to serve as principal in private and Christian schools as well.

As the years marched onward and I reflect on my childhood and adulthood, thankfulness to God and pride fills my heart. I went

22

from being a child who had to put cardboard in his shoes to keep his feet dry to principal and role model for a young elementary school boy who one day commented on my shoes, saying, "I like your kicks!"

Though society may have considered our family of thirteen children to be members of the underclass in our town, and though we were subjected to racial discrimination, our parents left a legacy of values, ethics, and self-esteem. They taught us that we should not carry hatred or malice in our hearts. They instilled a spiritual foundation that sustained us and helped us to prosper.

I learned early on that my parents somehow were always right. The values that my parents introduced to me are not principles that are taught in a classroom but instead learned every day at home. Some children grow up without having been provided with this necessary foundation for a successful life, but we were some of the "lucky ones." I am very thankful to my mother and father for shaping me into the man I have always dreamed of becoming.

Me and my siblings at the 1981 Family Reunion in Oakdale Park. Standing, left to right: George, Virginia (deceased), Wilma, Connie, Wilkie. Kneeling, left to right: me, Clifford (deceased), Frances, Norma (deceased), Roger. Not pictured: Arlene (deceased)

Good Teacher, what shall I do that I may
inherit eternal life? (Luke 18:18 NKJV)

Everyone loves to hear an old-fashioned, rip-roaring "glory" conversion testimony. For example, the person who was a member of the Crips, a meth dealer, and mob hit man before he found Jesus. Or the girl who grew up in a Christian home, then got involved in drugs, got pregnant, and then got saved. I believe these are powerful testimonies that cut right into the heart of the Gospel.

But many of us don't have a particularly gripping testimony. I grew up in a Christian home with a wonderful mom and dad. I had wonderful friends, never hung out with the bad crowd, never served time in a juvenile detention center, never robbed anyone, attended church and Sunday school every Sunday, and only occasionally got into fights with kids who would call me racial names. However, early in young adulthood, I realized that I needed Jesus just as much as everyone else.

My life paralleled the self-righteous man who said, "I have never murdered anyone, I've never been charged with stealing, I've never lied under oath," or "I've been a good son and have respected my parents." This man thought he had kept the commandments (Matthew 19:29) but knew he didn't have eternal life (Matthew 19:20). He knew he lacked something very important in his life. The Scripture points out that Jesus loved the rich young ruler and loved this man into the kingdom of God, showing how God both begins and brings to pass his work of salvation in an individual's heart (Philippians 1:6).

My born-again experience took place one evening during Bible study at the Harty Bible School. While studying the Scriptures, I learned that we are saved through faith by confessing sin and calling upon Jesus for eternal life. I did not have the assurance of everlasting life, and I felt a tugging in my heart to go forth and receive Jesus into my heart. The Bible teacher walked me through the following steps: "Acknowledge that you are a sinner" (Romans 3:23 NKJV); "Believe you will receive eternal life" (Romans 6:23 NKJV); and "Confess and believe" (Romans 10:9,13 NKJV). Being born again was a turning point in my life, a start in my spiritual journey when God unfolded his grand design for my life that led to total commitment for a lifetime of service to him.

CHAPTER 2

Family

He who finds a wife finds what is good
and receives favor from the Lord.
—Proverbs 18:22 NKJV

It is not good for a man to be alone, I
will make a helper suitable for him.
—Genesis 2:18 NKJV

IN 1968, GOD PLACED A beautiful woman of faith in my life when I started studying the Scriptures at the Harty Bible School at the Christian Tabernacle Church, where I was to become pastor many years later. After several months of dating, we seemed to know where

Joyce and I

God was pointing us and were ready to go with Him all the way to the marriage altar. We were pronounced husband and wife more than fifty-eight years ago.

Spiritually, my wife and I became deeply connected as we began serving in the ministry. In addition to being a faithful member alongside the other women in the church, she was also called upon to help the pastor with counseling for young women and served as a reading tutor to a young man in our congregation.

She served the Lord gladly and was a key figure in my life. I attribute my successes in Christian ministry, public and Christian schools, and our community and family to her as well.

God blessed us with the joy of raising three godly daughters, all of whom are living and serving the Lord. Our daughters, Andrea, Jennifer and Kelly, grew up to be mild-mannered and respectful with an esteemed view of their dad's calling.

After joyfully serving the Lord together for over three decades, God in His infinite wisdom showed me that He had other plans for my precious wife. She was no longer to remain here on earth but was to go to her heavenly home to celebrate her birthday with her beloved parents, sister, and brother.

Though her absence still pains me to this day, I take comfort in knowing that her presence made a difference in not only my life but so many others' lives as well.

Friends Forever

May our daughters be like graceful
pillars, carved to beauty a palace.
—Psalm 144:12 NKJV

Being a father of these three delightful daughters gave me an opportunity to serve as a board member for the YMCA's Indian Princess Program whose goal is to "form bonds that last a lifetime, so when your daughters enter the turbulent middle school and high school years,

Kelly, Andrea, and Jennifer

you have built a strong relationship and many precious memories."

My daughters and I are "Friends Forever." We have a close enduring relationship in which we enjoy each other's companionship and take the time to make memorable moments with each other. Many years have passed since the Indian Princess days, but I continue to share quality time and new bonding experiences with my daughters on a regular basis.

CHAPTER 3

When God Blocks Your Path

*And we know in all things God works for
the good of those who love him, who have
been called according to His purpose.*
                                    —Romans 8:28

S HORTLY AFTER ACCEPTING JESUS AS my Lord and Savior, I began
seeking God's will for my life. That is the ultimate question for
anyone thinking about serving God in any way, whether it's as pastor,
evangelist, missionary, or lay person. I felt it impressed upon me that
God wanted me to be a missionary to Liberia, West Africa.

God's Bible School and College in Cincinnati, Ohio enhanced
my gifts and equipped me for ministry. It inspired my passion for
missions and enriched my understanding of the Bible and Theology.

I graduated from God's Bible School and College with a
Bachelor of Art degree in Theological and Biblical studies. After
graduation from GBS, I enrolled in the School of Education at the
University of Cincinnati where I received a teaching certification,
thereby fulfilling the requirements to preach and teach as a missionary to Liberia, West Africa.

Three weeks before my family and I planned to sail for Africa,
we received heart-breaking news that a cancerous lump was found
in Joyce's breast. The medical procedure did not require chemo or
radiation. However, on the advice of our medical team, we were to
remain in the United States for a minimum of five years. My wife
and I were totally and utterly devastated.

Sometimes life brings circumstances you didn't plan for, so how do you handle it when God changes your plan? Although it was a tough pill to swallow, I needed to remind myself that our Sovereign God is in control of every aspect of our lives—even our disappointments. The manifestation of a promise of God may be delayed but His word tells us it not denied (2 Corinthians 1:20).

God redirected my life to serve as a teacher in the Pittsburgh Public schools. I was hired to teach 4th graders at Burgwin Elementary School in Hazelwood, Pennsylvania. Many times God's perfect will for me was evident during classroom sessions and interaction with students of whom I loved in the love of Jesus.

I spent the first seven years as a classroom teacher concurrently attending evening classes at the University of Pittsburgh where I received a principal certification, a Master of Art degree in Education, a Ph.D. in Supervision and Curriculum, and a Superintendent's Letter of Eligibility.

In our walk with the Lord, He uses our disappointments and heartbreak in stunning ways. He does it so that we may show and share the Gospel story with the world. God never promised that our lives would be easy, but if we are His, He does promise to use our disappointments for our good and His glory. His clock keeps perfect time. "Everything has its time, and everything that is wanted under Heaven has its time." (Ecclesiastes 3:1)

CHAPTER 4

Toward the Next Generation

The student is not above the teacher, but everyone
who is fully trained will be like their teacher.
—Luke 6:40 NKJV

I F YOU ATTENDED SCHOOL IN the 1960s, you know that things have changed as the decades roll by. What we taught and, in many cases, how we teach it has changed, but so have schools themselves.

You knew it would be a good day in school when teachers started rolling in the AV cart—this meant you were taking a break from the monotonous classroom lectures and watching a movie. Today, if teachers want to share a movie or video clip, they can simply stream it from the internet onto a screen or interactive whiteboard.

And just when you think that the classroom could not become any more modernized, school districts are upgrading the technology, which allows teachers to display computer screens and write notes directly onto the screen.

You may remember using the Dewey decimal system to find a book in your school libraries, only to find that other students had checked out all of the copies. But libraries serve a more varied purpose these days. Instead of checking out a book, more students are bringing their laptops to the library and using the space to write essays, research topics, and work on group assignments.

Growing up, you may have felt safest sitting in a classroom at school, but for today's generation of students, this is not the case.

Schools prepare seriously for emergencies by holding frequent lock-down drills. Students are taught not to open the door for anyone they don't recognize. Some schools even have metal detectors that students, staff, and visitors must walk through before entering the buildings.

If today's public school teachers want to force their students to stand for the Pledge of Allegiance, they should expect a lawsuit.

When you were in school, you were able to come and go freely from campus during open lunch or bring your parent in for a career day without being questioned. But with today's security concerns, this is not the case. Guests often need to sign in and obtain a visitor's pass from the main office.

Peanut butter and jelly sandwiches may have been a staple in your school cafeteria, but many of our schools have strict policies to protect students who suffer from food allergies. As a result, peanut butter and other allergens are not allowed to be served.

As schools begin to adapt to changing cultural attitudes and fluid representations of gender, gender-neutral bathrooms are appearing in school districts across the country.

The Common Core State Standards initiative does not mention cursive writing in its English and Language Arts section.

On June 25, 1962, the United States Supreme Court decided that prayer in a public school violated the First Amendment because it represented established religion. The decision by the Supreme Court to remove the Bible and prayer from our public schools may be the most spiritually significant impact in our nation's history over the course of the last fifty-five years.

Research conducted by the United States found five growing issues in the nation's public schools. Academic achievement has plummeted, including SAT scores; out-of-wedlock births, illegal drug use and juvenile crime have increased; and school behavior is deteriorating.

My First Teaching Assignment

As previously mentioned, my first teaching assignment began as a fourth-grade teacher at Burgwin Elementary School located in the steel mill community of Hazelwood located on the shores of the Monongahela River.

Burgwin Elementary School in Hazelwood

Fourth-graders are so alive! My students would rush down the hallways when arriving at school. They would unload their backpacks and coats in a frenzy (often dropping them unintentionally on the floor), push through the door, and into the classroom.

I remember saying to the class, "Okay, everyone, you're in fourth grade. We have to line up, walk through the halls quietly, hang your coats in your locker, come into the classroom, be seated, and get ready to start the school day."

I provided a behavioral management chart with classroom rules, rewards and consequences, which I posted and reviewed with the students. Classroom routines, including schedules and learning objectives, were set up and reviewed with the students so they could focus on learning.

Sometimes when I would go over the objectives and learning activities for the day, students would say things like "yes!" because they were excited by what we planned. Writing down and remembering these moments is such a reward.

Even well into the year, students often commented on the day with exclamations of delight. "Yes, we have PE today!" one student would exclaim while high-fiving his friend.

My students were taught to practice routines. Even if I didn't have lunch duty, I still taught my students how to navigate the cafeteria at the beginning of the year. I would take my class to lunch and make sure each one knew how to pay for lunch, how to carry a tray carefully, and how to find his or her seat.

We started the day with morning opening exercises that included flag salute, silent meditation, and announcements for the day.

All students kept personal multiplication charts in their math books so they could refer to them as they worked on longer multiplication and division problems. I gave an occasional fact quiz to check and see how they were doing as a class.

Fourth grade is an important transition year for students in reading. In earlier grades, they learn phonics, the correlation of sounds with letters and groups of letters. To determine their baseline, I used an assessment that included letter recognition, phonic awareness, decoding, and comprehension.

Expressing appreciation for students often elicits the same response in kind. Each day, as my students would leave, I would send them off with something to show I enjoyed them being in my classroom. On a regular school day, I might say something like "Goodbye! See you tomorrow!"

I would tell my students as they leave for the weekend, "Goodbye! I love you all! I'll see you in Sunday school." I was not only teaching them a valuable lesson in gratitude; they were giving me, in return, the reward of gratitude and consideration.

The school closed doors in 1990, because of a downsizing in student attendance, and reopened in 2000 as a Propel magnet school.

CHAPTER 5

Planting a Seed in Texas

I planted the seed, Apollos watered it,
but God gave the increase.
—1 Corinthians 3:6 NKJV

M Y DEGREES IN EDUCATION AND theology qualified me to serve in the fields of education as well as ministry. Shortly after graduating from God's Bible School and College, I accepted a call to a church plant in a predominantly African-American and Latino community northeast of Houston, Texas.

Joyce and I accepted the call, packed up our daughter Andrea, and moved to a city where we knew no one. We set out for Houston with the faith of Abraham and a desire to reach the unchurched. "By faith Abraham obeyed when he was called to go out to a place where he would receive as an inheritance. And he went out, not knowing where he was going" (Hebrews 11:8 NKJV).

Joyce, Andrea and I

I would need to find employment in order to supplement a stipend provided by the sponsoring church, so upon our arrival in Houston, I applied to the Northeast Houston School District and was offered a position as an elementary teacher. It was so amazing how the hand of God placed me in a school near the location of the proposed church plant.

Planting a church from scratch was a real challenge. We were to plant a church with no members, no building, no staff, no conferences, no training. and no physical church-planting manual, We knew the Word of God to be true that "one waters, one plants, but God gives the increase" (1 Corinthians 3:6 NKJV) and "unless the Lord builds the house, they labor in vain who builds it" (Psalm 127:1 NKJV).

One day, when conversing with the principal, he asked what brought me to Houston. I told him I was brought here by a church group to plant a church in Northeast Houston.

Shortly after the start of the fall term, the school held a "Meet the Teacher Night." Teachers were instructed to give a welcome-back-to-school speech for parents and students that included, among other things, sharing some details of our personal life. During the presentation, a parent raised her hand and asked, "What brought you to Houston?" I answered her the same way I had answered the principal.

A week later, I submitted a request to use the school gymnasium for Sunday worship services. The school board approved the request and blessed us with a place to begin services. The old adage holds true: "Where God guides, he provides."

Psalm 5:12 says, "For you, O Lord will bless the righteous with favor." We were uplifted, blessed, and thankful to God for providing an open door so we could begin church services.

Once the worship space was secured, we began developing strategies for organizing Sunday morning worship services. I planned and carried out a one-man door-to-door outreach—knocking on doors, inviting families to attend the Sunday service, and placing simple doorknob hangers where families did not answer the door.

We began preparing for the first Sunday service and were blessed when the school custodian volunteered to place chairs in the gym for the Sunday services each week. He was a born-again believer who attended a church in another part of town. Again, we were thankful and encouraged by the Word of God: "So you will find favor in the sight of man" (Proverbs 3:4 NKJV).

We grew excited as the first Sunday service was nearing. Finally, when the day came, we began with Sunday school, followed by a worship service with an attendance of three adults and four children. We began seeing a small increase each Sunday as I continued my one-man door-to-door visitations on Saturday.

One Sunday, in response to the altar call, a young mother named Vernell Pradia came forth and accepted Jesus Christ as her Lord and Savior. The following week, she brought her husband Michael, and he gave his heart to Jesus.

The couple had been living common law for a number of years. Now that they were saved, they were convicted and decided to get married. I had the privilege of performing the wedding ceremony in the living room of our home.

They became a husband-and-wife team that partnered with us in carrying out the Saturday visitations. In addition, they began inviting family members to the worship services. We began experiencing a move of God in our services as family members, neighbors, and children surrendered their lives to Jesus.

**Charter members of the church plant in Texas,
the Lockwood Church of the Nazarene**

We started a small midweek group session with discipleship training and evangelism. The study group partnered with the ministry by inviting people to the worship service. God honored their faithfulness by bringing several into a saving knowledge of Jesus Christ. They became members of our church and later held leadership roles as well.

We began seeking God's will for a building; the congregation began to increase, and they began expressing their interest in securing a building of their own. We held prayer meetings, began seeking existing buildings like empty schools, and even considered the possibility of constructing a building. The latter is where God eventually led us.

We shared the vision with our sponsoring church, Spring Branch Church of the Nazarene, and an affluent member donated a parcel of land with the stipulation that we show good faith in carrying forth and developing the church. The sponsoring church agreed to match any funds we raised for construction.

Our church members accepted the challenge and organized a building fund as an addition to our weekly tithes and offerings. The church was approved for 501(c)(3) tax exempt status by the IRS

The completed church, some years later after its construction.

which helped us to receive donations and allowed donors to receive tax deductions. We wrote a proposal and submitted it to a faith-based grant maker, requesting funding for the building project. The building project was awarded a substantial amount for the cost of building the structure, contingent on our ability to completely furnish the building.

God was faithful to multiply the building fund offerings through donations from church members, private organizations, and business owners. Finally, the building was constructed, furnished and recognized as a mission church of the sponsoring church.

A recent letter from Vernell Pradia, a charter member of the church states,

> *At the age of 29, I was living the good life, I had a good job working every day, but I was lost without Christ. I was living life in the fast lane, but the Lord had a purpose and plan for me. The Lord sent a couple to me, invited me to the school where services were being held every Sunday and my life took a turn for the best. I started hearing the truth. The truth is that I received Jesus Christ as my personal Savior and committed my life to Him. I began to witness Christ in a new way and invited my family and friends to attend church with me. Fifty-nine years have passed, and I am still living for the Lord, reading the Word, praying and witnessing to people about Jesus.*

CHAPTER 6

Out of Your Comfort Zone

*As an eagle stirs up its nest, hovers over
its young, spreading its wings, taking
them up, carrying them on its wings.*
—Deuteronomy 32:11 NKJV

WHEN AN EAGLE WANTS TO teach its eaglets to fly, it stirs up the
nest. The eagle brings the young eaglets out of the nest, picks
them up, flies to a high point, and releases them in the air. An eaglet
will never learn to fly until it's pushed out of the nest, which is its
comfort zone.

In the same way, when the Lord wants you to pursue a new
assignment, he wants to take you to a higher level in life. When he
wants to unleash your potential, he pushes you out of your comfort
zone and brings you into a new situation in which you are compelled
to use the abilities that lie within you.

Just when I was settling in as pastor of a growing young church
plant, I received a call from my home church to fill the pastorate
at one of the sister churches located in the steel mill community
of Aliquippa. We found it very difficult to leave our church family
whom we dearly loved, our beautiful refurbished home, and the pre-
school accommodations we had made for Andrea.

Since God knows the future, sometimes He has to remove us
from our comfort zone to a greater need in kingdom building. We
trusted and were obedient to the Lord because the ways of God are
not our ways. The first Sunday's church attendance at Christian

Lighthouse was only nine people. Subsequently, an outreach plan was put in place that consisted of much prayer, time, and effort to become effective.

Saturdays were devoted to house-to-house visitations; I picked up children in my car for Sunday school, planned a VBS, and canvassed the neighborhood on behalf of the church. Owens School Bus Company, which serviced the Aliquippa school district, later loaned us a bus for Sunday pickups in the neighborhood.

Members used their cars to drive people to and from church for Tuesday night prayer service and Sunday services as well. The Sunday school and church service began to grow in attendance with both young and old people giving their life to Christ. They became faithful, dedicated members of the church.

The Christian Lighthouse Church in Aliquippa

The church was in dire need of repair and renovation. The interior areas lacked room enough to accommodate our needs. God touched the hearts of George McCoy and Elias Tyler, two residents skilled in remodeling, who donated their time and secured building materials at a reasonable cost.

The church was not just a place of worship but a place where real ministry happened. The ministry was blessed with a community outreach in several ways, such as when a young son in the Lord, Gregory Person, installed a special telephone system that made it possible for sick and shut-ins to listen to Sunday services. There were also weekly street meetings; and a viable community-wide outreach ministry of Youth for Christ to young people in the community. A branch of the Harty Bible School was established with the partnership of the main school at Christian Tabernacle.

Although the ministry was reaching and blessing many families, it wasn't without tragedy and sadness. One Tuesday night, one of our faithful members was absent from the prayer service. I thought it was unusual for her to miss a midweek service but was told that her husband was taking her out for dinner. I knew of their domestic problems, but I reasoned with myself that perhaps it was an intended reconciliation.

After service, I drove home only to be met by my wife who frantically told me that a call came from the police department requesting that I identify the body of the church member who had been shot and killed in a wooded area by her husband. A few months later, the man took his own life while in jail.

A deadly accident occurred one evening while two members of the youth department were curiously examining a family-owned gun. The gun accidentally fired, striking one of the young men in the head and instantly killing him.

A mother of two of our regular Sunday school attendees was accidentally killed by a motorist who lost control of the car, causing it to run onto the porch of the house where she was sitting reading the newspaper.

Ministering during times of grief is a significant portion of the pastoral work of the church. God does not leave his children in the depths of sorrow. Joy comes eventually, and it comes in God's timing.

On the brighter side of the ministry, the church held annual Pastor Appreciation Sundays when the members, friends, and family gathered on the lawn after our service to set aside a special time for fellowship and food and to express their love and appreciation to me and my family.

Church vacation trips to Canada, Atlanta, Orlando, and Niagara Falls were always enjoyable times together as a church family. Annual church picnics were held at local parks, and marriage enrichment seminars were held at Gilmary Retreat Center in Center Township

After thirteen years of a blessed, rewarding pastorate, I transitioned to the pastorate of the Christian Tabernacle, the mother church in the city of Pittsburgh.

CHAPTER 7

Faithful in Little, Faithful in Much

*Well done, good and faithful servant! You
have been faithful in a few things. I will
put you in charge of many things.*
— *Matthew 25:23 NKJV*

I AM NOT SURE IF THERE is anything harder than being faithful in the little things. If God does indeed have something bigger in his plans for your life, you can be assured of one thing—you will not get it until you have been faithful in the little things that you have already been given. In the parable of the talents, Jesus teaches that if you are faithful in little things, one day God will entrust you to do more things. (Luke 16:10)

Christian Tabernacle's motto was "The hill district's center for missions and evangelism." It was a church that embraced sharing the Word of God to those who have not yet been reached with the Gospel in the community, the state, and the regions beyond.

The church's Foreign Missionary Board's vision was carried out by praying, recruiting, and training missionaries for service in Liberia, West Africa. Annual mission conferences were held to encourage, equip, and enlist workers for the missionary field. God faithfully raised up church members who served as foreign missionaries to Killingsworth Mission in Monrovia, the capital city of Liberia. I was blessed to minister four short-term summers there.

My initial feeling that I had work to do in the mission field was now coming to pass.

The Home Missionary Board under the direction of president Mazie Myles, supported the foreign board by making dresses for children in Liberia and assisting in packing foodstuffs in drums to be sent there.

They cared for those on the home front by sponsoring clothing drives and hosting annual Thanksgiving dinners for families and seniors in and around the Hill District of Pittsburgh. The missionary board supported the ministry by preparing the communion table with a supply of bread and grape juice, with freshly laundered coverings over the elements.

The church's prison outreach ministry, under the leadership of Russell Wells, was to reach lives for Jesus Christ behind prison walls. Throughout the Bible are examples, descriptions, and commandments about prisons, prisoners, bondage, captivity and slavery. The greatest scriptural mandate for prison ministry is given in Matthew 25:34. "I was in prison and you visited me." Monthly visitations were made to inmates at Muncy State Correctional Institution.

The church's position was that every believer should be involved in prison ministry. This does not necessarily mean you are called to actually go into a prison. As in missions, not everyone is called to a foreign field to share the Gospel. But as in missions, the church members were involved in the prison ministry in some capacity through prayer support for the ministry, visiting an inmate, writing to a prisoner, and assisting families of inmates.

Preacher/Teacher

The apostle Paul instructed Timothy, his son in the ministry, that mature Christian believers should be diligent to present themselves approved by God as a workman that need not to be ashamed, handling accurately the word of truth (2 Timothy 2:15 NKJV).

Handling God's Word accurately or "rightly dividing the word of truth," as the King James Version translates it, means interpreting the Bible text correctly. In more scholarly language, it means to practice good hermeneutics. Jesus chided the Pharisees of his day for their poor hermeneutics, saying, "You do not understand the Scriptures (Mark 12:24 NKJV).

The church's ministry of evangelism and education developed as a four-year Bible course for adults desiring a working knowledge of the Bible. As pastor of the church, I served as president of the Harty

The Harty Bible School

Bible School—named after John Walker Harty, a previous pastor of the church. I continued to teach, with Joyce serving as my assistant. We provided administrative support for staff and students, and oversaw the operation of the Bible school.

In addition to the core courses of the four-year study, the Harty Bible school offered supplemental and postgraduate courses in basic English and grammar, written and oral composition, prophecy, and teacher training.

The Bible school was open to persons of all faiths, denominations, levels of faith, and stations in life who desired to increase their knowledge of the Word of God as revealed in the Holy Bible, whether in preparation for a particular ministry or with a purpose of gaining knowledge for knowledge's sake.

The Bible school provided the new convert with a foundation in the Gospel, provided the believer with an answer to their quest for continued growth in the Word and provided all others with an analysis of the doctrine at the base of the Christian faith.

I finally retired after thirty-five fruitful years serving as teacher and president of the Harty Bible School. In Ezra 7, we learn that to have God's hand of blessing on us, we must study and obey His Word with a view of teaching others and glorifying God for everything.

The Christian Tabernacle is one of the churches that are under the denominational leadership of the supervising elder, the highest order in the Kodesh Church of Immanuel. The supervising elder is authorized and set apart by a two-thirds favorable vote of the general assembly and has jurisdiction and the oversight of all churches in the denomination. With a favorable vote of the general assembly of the churches, I received the honor of the office of supervising elder, succeeding the passing of Dr. Rev. Frank Russell Killingsworth, the ninety-eight-year-old church founder and supervising elder.

I accepted the position and worked tirelessly to carry out the duties of supervising elder while simultaneously serving as pastor, Bible school teacher and president, and ex-officio member of the general church auxiliaries and boards. By order of the office of supervising elder, I faithfully planned and supervised annual church conferences, traveled throughout the denomination visiting the churches to address temporal and spiritual matters, ordain deacons and elders, organize local churches, and place or replace pastors.

At the end of forty faithful years of Christian service, the denomination presented a plaque to me reading, "Well done good and faithful servant...your faithful service is an offering to God... He will not forget how you have shown your love to Him over the years...by caring for and ministering to others as you still do. We believe as long as you live, God has a purpose for you on earth. God still wants to use you for His glory "Be confident of this very thing, that He which hath begun a good work in you will perform it until the day of Jesus Christ" (Philippians 1:6 NKJV).

CHAPTER 8

Without Walls

*Take hold of instruction, do not let
go, guard her for she is your life.*
—*Proverbs 4:13 NKJV*

National Teacher Corps

IN THE MID-1960S, THE HIGH turnover of experienced teachers and absence of well trained teachers in largely minority and low-achieving schools was obvious. The belief driving policy makers and donors was that young, committed, and better trained teachers working in these schools could raise student academic levels, reduce high drop-out rates, and increase the number of high school graduates going to college.

After returning from Houston, I taught for a while at Knoxville Elementary School in the Knoxville section of Pittsburgh. Then I was assigned to Columbus Middle School on Pittsburgh's North Side. The National Teacher Corps Program was implemented at the school and I directed the program as team leader.

I was responsible for the supervision of teacher interns constituting a team. My duties included acting as liaison between the interns and university officials, coordinating and planning with the interns, demonstrating teaching techniques, overseeing individual and team activities, and evaluating their performance.

The teacher interns taught for half days under the supervision of master teachers, attended classes at Pitt and seminars on the site after school. At the end of the year the interns were certified to teach in the Pittsburgh Public Schools and earned a Master of Art degree in teaching.

Some of the interns became teachers in the Pittsburgh Public Schools. Others took jobs elsewhere teaching disadvantaged students, usually in their home states. But no matter where they taught, the lasting effects of having been a part of the Teacher Corp was evident.

Open Classrooms

The open-classroom concept was introduced into the United States in 1965 as an experimental elementary school architecture where the physical walls separating classrooms were removed to promote movement across class areas by teachers. However, in practice, this is not typical since teachers tend to teach in a traditional manner. It is derived from the one-room schoolhouse but sometimes expanded to include more than two hundred students in a single multi-age and multi-grade classroom.

Across the US, schools were designed and built with these new ideas, and the new approach to the learning that would take place inside of them. It was a response to the fear that the US was falling behind in key subjects like science and math. The approach resonated with those who believed that America's formal, teacher-led classrooms were crushing students' creativity.

It was common knowledge at the time that one of the city's premier schools, Carmalt Elementary, would be opening as an open-classroom magnet school in the fall, and teachers would be "handpicked." Surprised, and with honor, I was one of the lucky ones to be assigned as fifth-grade teacher and team leader.

Teaching in an open-space school presents challenges that are not faced when teachers are in individual classrooms. Classroom management was of the essence when several classes of students in one large area, (a "pod") are interacting with the teacher while other classes are in session.

Carmalt Elementary School

Concerted team effort was important in developing positive collaborative teaching relationships and comradery; daily team meetings were essential to discuss ongoing assessment data, differentiated teaching, and learning strategies.

Our instructional team developed ways that supported both the students' and the teachers' growth. While teaching, I attended Pitt evening classes, receiving an elementary principal certification. After five years of classroom teaching, I was appointed vice principal of the school. Sadly, during Christmas break, our principal suddenly passed away, and I was appointed acting principal.

CHAPTER 9

Deutschtown

*So also, unless you give understandable speech by
teaching, how will that which is spoken be known.*
— *1 Corinthians 14:9 NKJV*

A sign as you enter Deutschtown in Pittsburgh's North Side

I N THE UNITED STATES EDUCATION system, magnet schools are public schools with specialized courses or curriculum. "Magnet" refers
to how the schools draw students from across the normal boundaries
(defined by authorities as school zones) that tend to feed into certain
schools.

My aspirations to become an administrator landed me the posi-
tion of principal of a school mandated by the State of Pennsylvania
Department of Education to racially balance the school's 90 percent
African-American population.

The decision to open Manchester Elementary School as a
Deutsch Magnet Schule—a German magnet school, was based on historical data of German neighborhoods in two Northside communities—Deutschtown, a historical German neighborhood, and Troy
Hill, founded on strong German roots developed in the 1850s.

As part of the objectives, methods, goals, and activities, students
in grades one to five would receive the official German curriculum
for a total of 2 1/2 hours daily, in addition to required core subjects.

My preparation for effective leadership began by explor-
ing German courses of study prescribed by the Foreign Language
Department of the school district and enrolling in a conversational
German course at community college. I learned basics of the German
language and conversational phrases.

Meetings were held with community interest groups of leaders
and parents supportive of the German magnet program. One community leader was a pastor of one of the neighborhood churches
who expressed a high level of interest in the project. He informed
the committee of his connection with community leaders in Bonn,
Germany. A unanimous consensus of the community interest group
planned for me to visit a German school in Bonn, Germany.

I traveled to the Bonn International School in Germany, located
on a tree-lined suburb in the outskirts of Bonn City. It was situated
on the banks of the Rhine River, where the rich and cultural tra-
dition of Germany really comes to life. The elementary principals
at the school were bilingual, with roots in the United States. They
welcomed me, expressing their gratitude for my interest in traveling
to Bonn.

While visiting the school, I observed classroom instruction, met with administrators and teachers; reviewed curriculum; discussed delivery of instruction, grading procedures, and lesson planning; and shared ideas. We developed a network with the German teachers that would be ongoing with teachers at our school.

While preparing to return to the United States, the faculty and staff honored me with a picnic and bike ride along the majestic Rhine River. Needless to say, many lasting friendships were forged with the teachers and administrators in Bonn, Germany.

Manchester Elementary, the "Deutsch Magnet Schule"

The German Magnet Program was a tremendous success. The program balanced the school population racially and there was a waiting list of families wanting to come. The program brought families together from other neighborhoods; raised test scores; brought about high levels of self-esteem among the student body, teachers, and staff; and fostered and maintained academic excellence at every grade level.

I attribute the success of the school in part to our neighbors, parents, community (and church) leaders, teachers, and members of the school board. Our students used the opportunity to achieve incredible goals in their lives and their careers, for instance:

One of our fifth-grade girls, Ashley Battle, was the only girl on the boys' basketball team. While playing in an all-school tournament, a few athletic recruiters saw her and began recruiting her to play for them. She ended up playing collegiately for the University of Connecticut, was later drafted by the Seattle Storm, and played professionally for New York Liberty and San Antonio Silver Stars.

Another student, Lamman Rucker, became an actor, a career which began with his first role as Martin Luther King in the fourth grade. He has appeared on the daytime soap operas *As the World Turns* and *All My Children* and landed roles in Tyler Perry's films *Why Did I Get Married?* and *Meet the Browns*. He starred as Jacob Greenleaf in the Oprah Winfrey Network drama series *Greenleaf* from 2016-2020.

Eddie Benton became an American College Women's basketball coach. He is best known for his collegiate player career at the University of Vermont and was named the Frances Pomeroy Naismith Award winner in 1996.

Joey Ward excelled at math while in grades kindergarten through fifth grade at Manchester. He went on to graduate from the University of Denver with a degree in Finance and Economics, and later became an M&A associate at Exus Management Partners, an independent investment and asset management firm.

CHAPTER 10

More Than a Good Lesson Plan

He who walks in integrity and
moral character walks securely.
—Proverbs 10:9 NKJV

F OR ALMOST THREE DECADES, WHILE working as a classroom
teacher, principal, and superintendent of schools, I have witnessed how the power of a school environment that focuses on
character development can shape the attitudes and lives of children.
Some of the most rewarding aspects of my career have been in the
inner-city schools that were almost always associated with violence,
apathy, defiance, and poor academic achievement.

At Manchester Elementary, it seemed that as the community problems grew, the academic and social attitudes of students
declined. I wanted to not only educate the students academically, I
wanted to educate their hearts.

One of my first actions as the new principal was to design a
school environment that emphasized character development. It was
obvious to me that the standard formula of filling children with math
and reading skills did little to promote the very behavior they needed
to succeed in those subjects.

As a faculty, we began to discuss and plan lessons around concepts such as hope, respect, cooperation, honesty, trust, and all the
other basic human values that foster good citizenship. We established
value-oriented themes that tied together social studies, music, and art
and generally promoted the notion of "good citizenship" throughout

the school. Most importantly, we created an environment of respect, responsibility, and cooperation.

Teachers promoted these concepts in their classrooms through lessons and behavior modeling. I watched, sometimes in amazement, as many of our students grew into responsible members of our school community. Children began to accept more responsibility for their actions, and the school became more manageable.

There was a substantial increase in student achievement that had a multiplying effect as it increased self-esteem of the students. I also witnessed a dramatic decrease in the number of suspensions, office referrals, and student absences.

Another successful tactic we used was a whole-class discussion model. By generating class discussions based on a different charac-ter-building trait each month, the children became familiar with the vocabulary of values as well as actions or options to be taken to accept responsibility. Concepts such as kindness, courtesy, honesty, respect, commitment, and courage were defined and discussed.

As one teacher discussed the concept of courage, a child asked, "Do you mean I'm showing courage when I walk away from a fight?" The discussion continued and that truth was affirmed by teacher and students. It was a major paradigm shift for the child to realize that one could be courageous when one did not fight, con-front, or defy.

The experience of this discussion was shared by teachers at our weekly planning meeting. It was one of those emotional, even pro-found, times in teachers' careers when we knew we were making a difference. That conversation and others like it confirmed our sus-picion that the environment we were developing in our school was already paying dividends. We were on our way to building a strong school!

Of equal importance, I noticed a positive change in the atti-tudes of the faculty and staff. As teachers witnessed the improved atmosphere at the school, their self-confidence improved. They began to believe that they were making a difference in the lives of the children because this new approach to working in our school was producing positive results. Teachers transmitted a new energy to students, and the overall environment of the school changed from one of pessimism to one of hope and confidence.

Our teachers made every effort to model these concepts through their own behaviors. Teachers and students would talk about school and neighborhood incidents and suggest alternative strategies as to how to deal with a range of problems that confront these children in their daily lives both in and out of school.

The successful implementation of the character education program served as a model to the other schools in the district. To that end, I was appointed to serve as a consultant for the program and provided in-service training for other city and suburban schools.

CHAPTER 11

Today's Pupil, Tomorrow's President?

A wise man will hear and increase in learning.
—Proverbs 1:8 NKJV

BARBARA BUSH WAS THE FIRST lady of the United States from 1989 to 1993, as the wife of George H. W. Bush, who served as the forty-first president of the United States. After spending ten years traveling around the United States of America visiting literary programs, libraries, kindergarten groups, day-care centers, single-parent classes for high school dropouts, and public housing projects, it became very apparent to her that the problem of an illiterate America needed to be addressed.

Mrs. Bush believed in family, country, and the importance of literacy and education as foundational to living a life full of possibilities and opportunities. She took the opportunity to explore her passion and began the groundwork. Her commitment to the cause of literacy crystallized and launched the Barbara Bush Foundation for Family Literacy on March 6, 1989.

Barbars Bush enjoyed reading to students.

I was selected, along with other elementary principals, to spend one week at George Washington University, writing position papers that supported and outlined a school-wide family literacy plan to be considered an essential blueprint for the Barbara Bush Family Literacy Foundation.

School Superintendent Louise Brennen stated, "Ken has a track record of high-achieving early childhood programs as well as viable programs that provide opportunities for families to learn while being involved in their child's education."

Upon arrival at the university, we participated in a formal "meet and greet" followed by lunch with the First Lady, who was the keynote speaker for the afternoon session. She shared a passionate message of the need and importance of a nationwide literacy program.

She said, "A man once gave me some peonies and said 'if you plant them, first dig a deep hole, fertilize and spread the roots, and put the dirt back. They might not bloom the first year, but they will bloom for the next one hundred years.' That's the way I think about literacy—if you teach a mother and child to read, that family will read for hundreds of years to come, and I honestly believe that if more people could read, write, and comprehend, we would be that much closer to solving so many of the problems that plague our nation and our society."

The Barbara Bush initiative became The Foundation for Family Literacy, a nonprofit organization that seeks to provide funding to improve literacy in the United States.

CHAPTER 12

There is Nothing You Can't Do

Every place the sole of your foot shall
tread upon; I will give to you.
—Joshua 1:3 NKJV

O NE DAY, WHILE AT MY desk at school, a call came from the deputy superintendent of schools to discuss the board's decision to reopen an elementary school located in the West End side of town. It had been closed for ten years.

The superintendent informed me that I was her first choice for the job, stating, "Ken has demonstrated through the years the skills that we felt are needed to open a new school. He works with parents, community, and staff. He is the right man for the job."

West End parents concerned about drugs and violence in the nearby housing development had protested the school board's decision to reopen the school. The building was located in a community that, according to police statistics, had the highest crime rate in the city of Pittsburgh.

The protests stemmed from a concern for the physical safety of the children. The neighborhood around the school consisted almost entirely of public housing projects. Drug dealers, gang wars, crimes, and drive-by shootings were commonplace. Many community members gave little credence to the school's predictions that children would not be harmed.

Before accepting the position, I did a prayer walk around the building, gazing at boarded-up windows and walls filled with graffiti and chanting the words God gave to Joshua saying, "Every place that the sole of your foot shall tread upon; I will give to you as I promised to Moses." As I walked several times around the building with uplifted hands, I felt the peace of God confirming His Word to my heart. In obedience to God's bidding, I accepted the charge.

School in the West End before renovation.

To get the school ready, I moved into the closed school during late winter while it was still being renovated. The buzz of construction was going on, dust was flying, and empty booze bottles littered the schoolyard. I occupied a filthy, boarded-up office with no running water or heat.

As renovation progressed, I conducted tours for parents of prospective students. A husband and wife of a neighboring community were among the visitors who decided to transfer their daughter, stating, "The whole school shows the principal's dedication to children and parents."

A second-grade teacher with twenty-two years of experience, who worked with me at Manchester, transferred to the school. She remarked by saying, "He is a principal who didn't leave his classroom experience behind. He will go to bat for his teachers if he knows they've done their job."

A white first-grader that transferred said, "I followed Dr. Barbour because I like him, and he's a nice principal."

A parent was skeptical about the reopening until she heard that I was the principal. She enrolled her child in the early childhood program. Ironically, the parent remembered me as once being her fifth-grade teacher, stating, "One thing I remember from him was he taught us to have confidence in ourselves, and that there was nothing we couldn't do. We could do whatever we wanted with our lives. That's something I tell my kids now."

Another parent credits the school with helping her son who had self-management issues. The mother said the boy would run the halls, throw things, and even climb onto the school's roof. An evaluation diagnosed the child with an attention deficit disorder. Proper follow up procedures were put in place. "If it wasn't for Dr. Barbour, I wouldn't have known what to do," she said.

The school was named a "back to the basics" magnet school offering special instruction and programs not available elsewhere, designed to attract a more diverse student body from throughout the school district. Quite naturally, at the top of our list was curriculum development and its successful implementation.

The "back to the basics" curriculum was designed with an emphasis placed on reading, writing, creative thinking, math, science, and Spanish. All students were taught the fundamental principles of citizenship, discipline, respect, and personal responsibility. Our students saluted the flag each morning and had silent meditation in each classroom.

The school board adopted school uniforms for all students in order to put low-income students on an equal footing with other children. Our teachers enforced discipline as a team, and there was no tolerance for any forms of misconduct, violence, or substance abuse.

New furniture and equipment for the school was obtained, and a special room was built off the library where students could read stories to one another. The school environment was enhanced by an artist at the Carnegie who designed colorful banners that extolled school-wide themes based on values and character development. Hallway banners were fashioned to announce our intent, and classrooms were decorated with signs and slogans that strongly encouraged such valued human traits as honesty, courage, cooperation, respect, and responsibility.

We worked hard to recruit students, particularly white youngsters, into the predominantly black neighborhood. In the end, 54% of the students were black, 46% white. Originally, 155 students in Grade K-5 and seven staff members were assigned to the school. Some of the students came from intact families, while others came from unstable homes, and for them, the school had to take on a parental role.

The school was made safe with a full-time in-school security guard. School doors were locked after the children entered the building, and parents and visitors used a buzzer system to gain entrance to the building. The pride of neighborhood parents and community leadership reentered the learning community.

Because of leadership that won the respect of parents, teachers, and those who once skeptically held scant hope for the school's success, students began to thrive in an emotionally, physically secure, strong academic environment and consistently scored high above local and national standards in reading, math, and science.

Staff and students pose outside of West Side Traditional Academy

The West Side Traditional Academy was filled with proud children, excellent teachers, a racially balanced population, and a waiting list of parents anxious to have their children become part of an exciting academic school experience.

There isn't anything that we can't do. With God's help, we can scale any wall and conquer any challenge while standing on His Word. One of the great stories in Scripture is that of Joshua. It's a story of leadership, courage, and faith that we can apply to our lives today—to trust Him in all things in the most impossible situations in our lives.

"Be strong and courageous for you shall cause the people to inherit the land." This is the foundation block upon which the West Side Traditional Academy was built. I thank God for His faithfulness, keeping his promise that "every place the sole of your foot shall tread upon I will give to you."

CHAPTER 13

Don't Follow Your Heart—
Follow Jesus!

*For my thoughts are not your thoughts, neither
are your ways my ways, declares the Lord.*
—Isaiah 55:8 NKJV

*So, though your heart will try to shepherd you
today, do not follow it. Remember, your heart only
tells you what you want, not where you should go.*
—John Piper

HOW DO WE KNOW IF a certain career path that we choose to enter is "God's perfect will" or "God's permissive will?" I believe his "permissive" will is anything which God permits you to do whether or not it is best for you, or even pleasing to Him!

In the "permissive" will of God, you are vulnerable to any attack by Satan. It is my belief that he will look at the slightest mistake on your part to attack you at these times. God's perfect will is where your blessing is located, and you will be glad to be in it.

I applied for the position of superintendent in the Wilkinsburg School District, a neighboring predominantly African American inner-city school district. When asked why I wanted to become superintendent, I replied, "Because of my successful record of positively touching lives of students in our school district, I wanted to become a school superintendent where I would have the opportunity not only to touch lives of school-aged kids, but also the community at large."

While serving as school superintendent, I faced some challenging experiences. It came as a surprise to me to learn that the district had a full-blown effort underway to privatize one of the elementary schools in the district. I found it hard to imagine that anyone would want to turn public money over to a stream of corporate profiteers with no education background.

A school in the Wilkinsburg School District

I knew that state law required that in order to earn a Pennsylvania teaching certificate, all candidates for certification are required to hold a bachelor's degree or must attend a teacher education program approved by the Pennsylvania Department of Education. It was unlawful to issue teaching certificates to people who do not meet state standards. The whole "privatizing effort" became a disaster and was subsequently closed down.

The day-to-day functions of school superintendent soon overwhelmed my ability to have positive interactions with teachers, students, parents, and community. I realized it was not what I wanted for my career.

It may be that we need to close a door so God can open a window. Scripture provides us with an abundance of short, sharp, and serious verses that God intends for us to hide in our hearts. When God closes a door, he opens a window that accurately captures what Scripture teaches about God's providence in our lives. "The heart of man plans his way, but the Lord establishes his steps" (Proverbs 16:9 NKJV). When your mind is at peace, it's easy to detach yourself from the past and see more clearly the "new window" that opens for you as a "new face in the community."

CHAPTER 14

A New Face in the Community

Many are the plans in the mind of man, but
it is the purpose of the Lord that will stand.
—Proverbs 16:9 NKJV

God shows no partiality, and does what is right
and acceptable to him. He looks at the heart and
not on the outward appearance of man or woman.
—1 Samuel 16:7 NKJV

THE BIBLE IS CLEAR THAT God is no respecter of persons and salvation has never been about race, but about grace. After resigning at the Wilkinsburg School District, I officially took the reins of principal at Tenth Street Elementary in Oakmont, a predominantly white school where I was the first African American administrator in the school district.

The racial demographics of the community population were 97.56% white, 0.71% black, and less than one percent Hispanic or Latino. Average household income today is $90,807, median house value, $191,200. Oakmont is considered one of the best places to live in Pennsylvania.

A concern among parents, teachers, and community leaders was the quality of leadership that would be provided by an African-American principal, whose experience was in predominantly black schools in the inner city.

The superintendent stated, "Our community is in the great position of having a fully qualified and prepared individual ready to step into the role of principal of one of our district schools." He further stated, "Dr. Barbour's years of experience and the positive relationships he has forged in previous assignments within school communities provide a valuable asset to our district."

Tenth Street Elementary in Oakmont

As we walk through our professional life, God puts special people in our path; people who show us the meaning of friendship, love, and compassion. For me these special people are the teachers, students, parents, and community officials of this school district where I served as elementary principal. My years were fruitful, fulfilling, and produced lasting friendships.

During my tenure as principal, I received many kind expressions from students, parents, and teachers alike.

Dr. B is special because he helps you. He's a nice man, and he cares about you all the time. He is a good principal at Tenth Street School. He watches over you all the time. He is a very good friend.
—First-grade student

Dear Dr. B, thank you for your help with Jack yesterday. You really made my day (and his) a lot easier. My husband and I have been impressed with your commitment to academic excellence and your discipline policy. But yesterday, you went well beyond the call of duty, and we will always remember your kindness. I hope that you realize how lucky most parents feel that you are our principal. You have our fullest support.
Sincerely, Peggy Donahue
Parent

Dear Dr. B, thank you for your support and encouragement in getting me through a difficult day.
Sincerely, Carolyn Cicero
Teacher

Dear Dr. B, I want to thank you for helping me when my aunt died. I really appreciated that you cared about me as a real person, not as a child. Whenever I needed to talk to you, you were there. Even when I was wrong, you gave me the benefit of the doubt. It is nice to know that you are a smiling principal, not a mean one. I really enjoy having you for a principal. Thank you for everything you have done for me.
Thank you, Robert Dold
Student

Dear Dr. B, I just wanted to thank you for what you did for me this year. You have always been fair and understanding. You sort out the problem before it gets worse. You have helped me to get where I am today. Most of all, you had faith in me.

—Student

Dear Dr. B, I would like to thank you for the excellent leadership that you have brought to our school. The school gets better all the time because you are at the helm. You bring leadership and order. There is a sense that you are in charge and that you care very deeply about the school environment. The students, teachers, and parents respect you and they like you too. The school and the community of Oakmont are so lucky to have you. The difference that you make in our children's lives makes our jobs as parents that much easier.

Sincerely, Ginny and Mark Koenig
Parents

Dear Dr. B, I have the distinct pleasure of knowing you during the past four years that my daughter has attended Tenth Street School. In my professional life, I have had occasion to represent a number of school districts and interact intensively with many fine school administrators; however, I have yet to come across one that can match your ability and character. You are the finest school principal I have ever met.

—Parent

CHAPTER 15

From Manicured Lawns to Muddy Roads

*Declare His glory among all nations, His
marvelous deeds among the people.*
—*Psalm 96:3 NKJV*

FOR STUDENTS, SCHOOL WAS OUT for the summer. For me, however, I continued my mission of bringing about a better education for children.

I left for Cuttington University College in Liberia, West Africa. It was a transition leaving the manicured lawns in the suburbs of our city to the muddy roads in Liberia.

Friends of Liberia is a 501(c)(3) nonprofit organization, based in Washington, DC, whose mission is to rehabilitate the nation through the training of the country's educators and to ensure that students in Liberia have an opportunity to access excellent education.

Liberia had been two years into recovery from a seven-year civil war that devastated the nation and its educational system. Schools were closed during the conflict, leaving thousands of children without a means to education. School buildings had been destroyed, teachers fled the country, and many others didn't have chance to finish their education.

Friends of Liberia initiated Project LEAP (Liberia Education Assistance Program), that recruited United States teachers and administrators to travel to Liberia to train the country's educators in age-appropriate teaching methods.

I was given a special opportunity to work with a group of five other educators from across the United States to volunteer our time, talent, and resources to help the beleaguered country's elementary school get reestablished. As a member of LEAP, I had the privilege of training teachers at Cuttington University in Liberia to handle the demands of laying an educational foundation for the country's children after the war.

The college building was just a shell of its former self, but the desire of its students to learn to become better teachers was strong despite the war.

From Manicured Lawns to Muddy Roads

The team and I conducted workshops for thirty Liberian elementary school principals and primary teachers. We spent three weeks working on teaching methods, lesson planning, and administrative skills. In addition, I concentrated on how to build school management and put together effective lesson plans. I even taught English as a second language. Although Liberia is an English-speaking country, there are many different dialects.

My family waited anxiously to hear from me since there weren't any cell phones, and we were fifty miles into the interior of West Africa. Upon returning home, my daughter who was three years old said she would watch the yellow phone in our kitchen every day for a call from Daddy.

Even though this trip was not a religious mission, it was still very important to me. Faith is acted out in who we are and the giving of ourselves to others.

My religious mission trips to Liberia in 1976, 1983, and 1989 were to serve as a short-term missionary in the Todi District of Liberia, West Africa.

The team and teachers we were training.

CHAPTER 16

A New Season

There is a set time and a set season for everything
that the Lord has in store for you in life.
—Psalm 102:13 NKJV

MOVING INTO A NEW SEASON does not mean we need to forget
the old. Instead, we move on toward the next place God takes
us, and we build upon the blessings He has already given us. When
ordained doors swing wide open and everything is falling in place,
you will know at that time that it is your season, and it is your time.
God's Word tells us, "To everything there is a season, and a time to
every purpose under Heaven" (Ecclesiastes 3:1 NKJV).

The simplest, most effective path for success is the opportunity for an education. Why? Education transforms lives. Education
directly affects children's sense of well-being. Kids gain knowledge
and skills that will help them not only in college, but in the work-
place. When a child begins and stays in school, he or she changes the
course of not only their own life but that of future generations.

Education lights every stage of the journey to a better life, especially for the poor and the most vulnerable. To unlock the benefits of
education, all children need the chance to complete not only primary
school but also middle and secondary school. Education needs to be
high-quality so that children actually learn. Given education's trans-
formative power, it plays a central part in our global development
framework.

Today, education is undergoing change at an unprecedented rate. To prepare students to succeed in the global economy, they need new skills taught in new ways. Teachers need to develop new material and deliver it differently. Parents expect greater involvement, and administrators need to constantly improve administrative and management efficiencies.

We are living in what some have labeled the "post-Christian age," which is waging an all-out attack in order to win young people's hearts and minds. Secular faces are winning on many fronts, including in education. Private Christian schools are one of the ways parents can provide their children an education that doesn't run contrary to the morals and values they learn at home. One of the major advantages of Christian education is that they teach academics within a Biblical worldview.

Teaching Minds, Training Hearts

After my retirement from forty years of public education, I began to seek God's will for a new season of Christian ministry in my life. I was led to apply for the position of substitute teacher at Hillcrest Christian Academy in my home community of Bethel Park. While being interviewed by the human resource person, I was made aware that the school was in search of a principal. Based upon my experience and skill set, the position was offered to me.

I eagerly accepted, grateful that I could make a difference in a school with a Biblical worldview. I began reviewing Bible curriculum, textbook curriculum (with an eye on consistency throughout the grade levels), student achievement test scores, teacher certification, parental involvement, daily staff devotions, student chapel services, technology, staff development, and physical plant. We organized a team of teachers who assisted in developing a set of school-wide standards to be put in place at the beginning of the year and evaluated in the springtime.

The curriculum, at that time for K-8 students, was reviewed and accredited by the Association of Christian Schools International and the Middle States Association of Colleges and Schools.

Hillcrest Christian Academy in Bethel Park

As the school continued to grow and attract students, a number of physical, academic, and athletic improvements were made to the building. The athletic program was robust—offering basketball, volleyball, baseball, soccer, and track and field.

A high school-sized gymnasium was completed in 2007, and in 2010, Hillcrest began its high school program with four students whose parents were committed to the idea of Christian education.

Throughout my career, I had never administrated a high school, but I took on the project with relish, reviewing the course schedules and curriculum of several neighboring school districts. At first, our four fledgling high-schoolers (and the ones that followed in subsequent years) took some classes in vacant office spaces or repurposed elementary classrooms. But with the birth of the high school came the birth of a vision for a new building that would house the high school permanently.

In 2015, I presided over the ribbon cutting ceremony for the new building, which included a fully equipped science lab and seven new classrooms.

In 2016, I made the decision to retire from education and begin spending my time on other interests. In the interim, the school expanded its options and began offering college-level classes in partnership with Geneva College and Carlow University.

In 2021, when a newly-hired principal at the Academy suddenly resigned before he could take the reins, the school board of HCA asked me to step in as Interim Principal until a new permanent principal could be found. As I write this, it is here where I find myself, back in familiar surroundings, doing what I have always loved to do.

CHAPTER 17

Transforming Lives in the Community

Am I My Brother's Keeper?
—Genesis 4:9 NKJV

A COMMUNITY IS A GROUP OF people with common interests and values. A community is characterized by "wholeness" incorporating diversity and sometimes including people of different ages, ethnicities, educational background, and incomes.

Community responsibilities are an individual's obligations to the community and require cooperation, respect, and participation.

In a general sense, the term "brother's keeper" does not just mean being responsible for the welfare of a biological brother or sibling; its scope is extended to all human beings, regardless of race, culture, or religious background.

Jesus is our "brother's keeper." He is the good shepherd who laid down his life for his sheep (John 10:10 NKJV). Jesus has given us an example to follow in serving our brothers. "For I have given you an example that you should do as I have done to you" (John 13:15 NKJV).

When we talk about servanthood, we talk about caring for other people; we talk about meeting the needs of others before our own. We focus on what God sees in the world, and not what we see within ourselves. Being able to first seek out a brother's need is the very first step in becoming a servant leader. We need to understand what brotherly love is so that we can take care of our neighbors.

To this end, I served our community as captain of the Neighborhood Crime Watch program. The program was an organized group of citizens devoted to crime and vandalism prevention within our neighborhood. The aim of the program was to achieve safe and secure neighborhoods through the training of citizens who would monitor activity within the community. When a criminal activity was suspected, captains were encouraged to report to authorities, not to intervene on their own.

"Ears to hear and eyes to see—both are gifts from the Lord." (Proverbs 20:12 NKJV) With this training, and given specific information as to ongoing criminal activity, I could more readily be the extra "eyes and ears" we needed to effectively police our community.

Transforming Lives on a Cold Winter Day

It was one of the harshest days of the winter when students stepped from their busses to a warm building, began their opening exercises with their teacher, followed by my morning greeting to students. While sitting at my desk that day at the West Side Traditional Academy, I glanced through the window and saw a woman and a young child at the bus stop.

My first thought was that the child missed her school bus. Should I call transportation and have the bus circle back for the child? Well, this was not the case of a child missing a school bus, as I soon found out when I went out to inquire of the mother.

It seems that her daughter was sick during the night and was no better by morning. She was waiting for a bus, intending to get her child to the hospital for treatment. A public bus ran through the neighborhood, but not that often. The bus route to the hospital would mean riding the bus to the city and transferring to another bus to the hospital.

On days like this one, a child cannot stand at a bus stop for longer than ten minutes without the chance of getting frostbite. With that in mind, I volunteered to drive the mother and child to the hospital.

While driving back to school, I became consciously aware that no medical facilities were available to families in the community. I felt a strong tugging in my heart to establish a community health center staffed by a doctor with allied health professionals, for families in my school community.

I shared my vision with teachers, staff, school board members, church leaders, and community leaders. All were of one mind in unanimous support of the project. A committee was formed that included members of the citizen's cooperative, city worship and service centers, teachers, staff, and the school nurse.

The committee was to oversee the project and assist in proposal writing to secure funding for the project. A "Health Tomorrow" grant proposal was written and submitted to several funding sources.

The proposal was accepted by the Highmark Foundation with a grant that included all the funding for a completely furnished health clinic, staffed by volunteer doctors and nurses and providing health services at no cost to the families that lived in the community.

Mothers would no longer have to stand in the wintry weather with their sick child and travel by public transportation across town for medical care. A community health center was within walking distance, located right on the campus of the school.

Transforming Lives of Senior Citizens

I will still be carrying for you when you are old.
Your hair will turn gray, and I will still carry
you. I made you and will carry you safely.
—Isaiah 46:4 NKJV

Christians have a responsibility to show kindness, respect, and a sense of duty to the elderly. Yes, we are to respect all people, but there is a certain type of respect that we are to give to the elderly unlike our own age group.

I served as a board member of Prime Time Adult Care, an outreach ministry in my community. The program is a five-day-a-week program licensed by the Pennsylvania Department of Aging.

The goal of the program is to activate, reinstitute, or maintain function of the elderly to the greatest extent of their ability, thereby adding to their quality of life. With this help, individuals are able to remain at home for a longer period of time—thus delaying the costly emotional stress of twenty-four-hour residential settings.

The Prime Time Adult Care building in Bethel Park

While the elderly participate in the program, their caregivers receive the respite time that is so necessary to their physical and emotional well-being.

The program includes a separate unit for individuals who experience symptoms of emotional anxiety, or for those who need greater staff assistance than can be accommodated in the larger group or the original unit.

CHAPTER 18

Transforming Lives in My Family

*I will heal their backsliding, I
will love them freely.*
—*Hosea 14:4 NKJV*

MOTHER WANTED US TO BE good people—be kind and generous and honorable. She wanted us to get along with one another, care for one another, and stand up for what is right. She wanted so many good things for us, but more than anything else, her deepest desire for us to continue to believe in Jesus for our salvation and always follow his leading in our lives. My sisters, brothers, and I had a high standard of living for the Lord during our childhood, teenage, and high school years. We knew what it was to live a Christian life growing up as a young person.

When mother died, she had little to pass on to her siblings financially, but we do treasure the years of prayers that she stored up for us and especially for bringing all of us back to the Lord. She prayed for a long time for those that had wandered; that they would come back to the Lord. She kept praying and believing that God would work in their lives.

Ministering to your family is a crucial part of your service to God. The Scriptures places a high emphasis on family as one's first priority. In 1 Timothy, the young pastor is given sure advice by the aged apostle Paul on how to serve in the ministry. It is no surprise that one finds the words, "But if any provide not for his own, and specially, for those of his own family, he hath denied the faith, and is worse than an infidel" (1 Timothy 5:8 NKJV).

The Old Testament uses the term *backslide* to speak of those who have been near to God but have allowed sin to take them away from him. After high school, some of my siblings entered the workforce, others went to college, while some joined the armed forces, and others married. Some once knew the Lord earlier in their lives and then over the years grew further and further away from Him. As a result of chasing after their own fleshly lusts and/or falling into various types of sins, they knew were going against the will and ways of God.

There is nothing more heartbreaking than having a brother or sister whom you've grown up with, went to Sunday school and church services with, and whom you sang in the choir with, only to watch them go from living a life that is pleasing to the Lord to walking away from it in order to satisfy some worldly pleasure.

But not only is our God a God of big miracles, He is also a God of second chances. God loves to bring His people back when they have gotten away from Him, build them up, and fully restore them on the path of His perfect will for their lives.

My Brother Comes Back

> For whoever calls on the name of
> the Lord shall be saved.
> —Romans 10:13 NKJV

One evening, while teaching at the church Bible school, I received a message that my youngest brother, Clifford, was in critical condition at a hospital in Houston, Texas. The hospital requested a family member to come immediately to his bedside. While hastily packing my carry-on bag with the bare necessities, I neglected to include my Bible.

Upon arriving in Houston, I checked in at a hotel close to the hospital, got a room key, and headed to the room. While unpacking a few things from my carry-on bag, I glanced at the nightstand and saw a beautiful King James Bible. The Bible was one of the one million Bibles distributed by Gideons International, an association of Christian businessmen who are dedicated to distributing God's Word around the world. Complete Bibles are left in hotels and motels, and New Testaments are provided to middle schools, high schools, colleges and many other places.

I knew immediately it was an answer to prayer, for truly, God is faithful to His Word and His promises. In the book of Isaiah, God says, "I will answer you before you call to me, while you are still talking about your needs, I will go ahead and answer your prayer" (Isaiah 65:24 NKJV). I remember hearing folks use the old adage, not from the Bible, saying, "God is never late, never early, but he's right on time."

I arrived at the hospital and was made aware that Clifford's condition was serious and would soon result in death. While at his bedside, I asked him about his walk with God and if he was living for the Lord as in the days of our youth. He admitted that he had gotten away from the Lord by putting other things first and wasn't sure of his salvation. My response was "You can be sure today of your salvation."

I told him that we were going to take a walk on the "Romans Road to salvation," which is based on Biblical principles found in the New Testament book of Romans. I used the Scriptures and walked him through the necessary steps to receive saving faith in Jesus Christ, "that whoever calls on the name of the Lord shall be saved." My brother took every necessary step to salvation and gave his heart to Jesus. A few days later, he passed away, but not before telling his girlfriend, "Kenny got me saved today."

Sisters Gets Saved

One day, while visiting my older sister Connie whom I walked closely with during the untimely tragic deaths of a son and a daughter, I offered a prayer and shared some encouraging Bible verses. It was at that time that she expressed to me that she wanted to get baptized. I

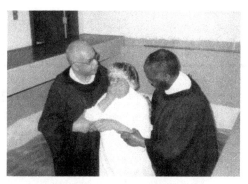

Baptizing my sister Connie

started by explaining that baptism symbolizes a person's dying to his or her past course of life and beginning a new life in Christ Jesus. She accepted Jesus as her personal Savior and blessed me with the joy of baptizing her at a Good Friday evening service in 1997.

On another occasion, I received a phone call from my sister Elaine, who lived in Dayton, Ohio. She had great news telling me she gave her life to Christ and was being baptized the following Sunday. At the close of our Sunday morning service my brother, George a licensed pilot and I flew to the church and witnessed her baptism. Years have passed and she continues to live for the Lord. She is a blessing to family and friends, and we appreciate her walk with God.

CHAPTER 19

Messages of Hope

For God did not give us a spirit of fear, but
of power and of love and of a sound mind.
—2 Timothy 1:7

FRIENDS, FAMILY, AND NEIGHBORS HOLD a special place in my heart, not just because of the good times we share but also for the bonds that are formed when we go through pain and adversity, holding each other up. There are people in my life whom I count as loyal friends and family that I dearly love. They may be young or old, close or distant, but no matter what, they hold a special place in my heart.

On March 11, 2020, the World Health Organization announced that the spread of the coronavirus (COVID-19) had become a pandemic.

During the COVID-19 pandemic, I was led by the Lord to write monthly messages to family and friends with a vision to help strengthen their faith in this unprecedented time and to encourage them on how to keep their trust in God during this global pandemic. Whoever and wherever they are, the messages of encouragement were intended to exercise "faith over fear, wisdom over worry, and prayer over panic, and to experience the peace of God, which surpasses all understanding" (Philippians 4:7 NKJV).

The messages contained Scriptures, words of affirmation, and quotes, and it was my prayer that these words would bring blessings to my family and friends and inspire them in a difficult time.

We could consider the COVID-19 vaccine as an early Christmas present from our scientific and medical communities. Let us thank God for men and women in the health-care professions whom God in his grace has given great skill, and to the thousands of clinical trial volunteers who risked their health to test an experimental vaccine for the benefit of others.

ABOUT THE AUTHOR

D R. KENNETH BARBOUR WAS THE tenth out of thirteen children born to a Pittsburgh coal miner, whose mother performed domestic work. Despite growing up poor and suffering from racial discrimination on a daily basis, Ken's parents always taught their children to never harbor hatred in their hearts. Ken states that this lesson has enabled him to not only succeed in life but also strive to touch hearts and lives of all races of people throughout his lifetime. Ken accepted Jesus Christ as his Savior after high school graduation. In the years that followed, Ken earned a master's degree in Christian ministry, a master's degree in elementary education, principal certification, and PhD in educational leadership. Ken's degrees qualified him to serve in many different capacities such as pastor, president (of a citywide Bible school), supervising elder (over the denominational churches), teacher, principal, and school superintendent. He was also afforded the opportunity to work with a variety of different people from lower class, inner-city residents to upper-class suburbia. After forty years of service in the public school system, Ken retired and accepted a position as principal of a predominantly upper-middle-class Christian academy for twelve years, and that is when he made the difficult decision to retire completely. Still eager to impact the lives of others and help them succeed as he has, Ken now spends his time teaching English as a second language at his daughter's piano and tutoring center. In addition, he serves as mentor to principals of two Christian schools on a needed basis.

www.ingramcontent.com/pod-product-compliance
Lightning Source LLC
Chambersburg PA
CBHW031711210125
20607CB00045B/818

* 9 7 8 1 6 3 8 7 4 4 8 4 9 *